WITHDRAWAL

Apréndete tus números/Know Your Numbers

Un gran edificio

Un libro para contar sobre construcción

One Big Building

A Counting Book About Construction

por/by **Michael Dahl**

ilustrado por/illustrated by **Todd Ouren**

traducción/translation: **Dr. Martín Luis Guzmán Ferrer**

PICTURE WINDOW BOOKS
a capstone imprint

Special thanks to our advisers for their expertise:
Stuart Farm, M.Ed.
Mathematics Lecturer
University of North Dakota, Grand Forks

Susan Kesselring, M.A.
Literacy Educator
Rosemount–Apple Valley–Eagan (Minnesota) School District

The editor would like to thank Donald E. Wolf, P.E.,
for his expert advice in preparing this book.

Editor: Brenda Haugen
Spanish Copy Editor: Adalín Torres-Zayas
Designer: Nathan Gassman
Book Designer: Eric Manske
Production Specialist: Jane Klenk
The illustrations in this book were created digitally.

Picture Window Books
151 Good Counsel Drive
P.O. Box 669
Mankato, MN 56002-0669
1-877-845-8392
www.capstonepub.com

Printed in the United States of America in North Mankato, Minnesota.
032010 005740CGF10

 All books published by Picture Window Books
are manufactured with paper containing at least
10 percent post-consumer waste.

Library of Congress Cataloging-in-Publication Data
Dahl, Michael.
    [One big building. Spanish & English]
    Un gran edificio : un libro para contar sobre construcción / por Michael
Dahl = One big building : a counting book about construction / by
Michael Dahl.
        p. cm.—(Picture window bilingüe, bilingual) (Apréndete tus números =
Know your numbers)
    Summary: "A counting book that follows the construction of a building,
from one plan to twelve stories. Readers are invited to find hidden numbers
on an illustrated activity page—in both English and Spanish"—Provided
by publisher.
    ISBN 978-1-4048-6294-4 (library binding)
    1. Building—Juvenile literature. 2. Counting—Juvenile literature. I. Title.
II. Title: One big building.
TH149.D3418 2011
513.2'11—dc22   2010009872

ONE big plan for making a big building.

UN gran plano para hacer un gran edificio.

!

Plan 3

2

TWO shovels dig a giant hole.

DOS palas mecánicas para hacer un hoyo gigantesco.

THREE dump trucks haul away the dirt.

TRES camiones de volteo
para acarrear tierra.

FOUR pile drivers pound
steel into the ground.

6

CUATRO martinetes clavan
columnas de acero en el suelo.

4
· · · ·

7

FIVE concrete mixers
rumble and roll.

8

CINCO mezcladoras de concreto
ruedan y retumban.

5

6

SIX metal beams are
lifted by a crane.

SEIS vigas de metal
levanta la grúa.

SEVEN workers sit in the shade and take a break.

SIETE trabajadores se sientan en la sombra y se toman un descanso.

EIGHT bosses worry that the weather will turn bad.

14

OCHO jefes preocupados porque puede hacer mal tiempo.

NINE wheelbarrows carry supplies.

NUEVE carretillas llevan materiales.

17

TEN windows reflect the sky.

DIEZ ventanas reflejan el cielo.

ELEVEN painters finish
the rooms and hallways.

ONCE pintores terminan las
habitaciones y los pasillos.

21

Fun Facts

 Before anything can be built, the soil needs to be cleared away for the building's foundation. The foundation supports the whole building!

 The world's tallest free-standing structure is the CN Tower in Toronto, Ontario. This tower is 1,815 feet (533 meters) tall!

 Many people are needed to make a building complete. They include carpenters, electricians, plumbers, painters, and many others.

Find the Numbers

Now you have finished reading the story, but a surprise still awaits you. Hidden in each picture is one of the numbers from 1 to 12. Can you find them all?

1 – middle window on bottom floor of plan
2 – ready to be scooped up by right shovel
3 – in the front wheel on the farthest right truck
4 – just below the reel for the cable on the pile driver that is farthest left
5 – on the boot of the worker emptying his cement truck
6 – at the top of the crane's cable
7 – the handle of the blue and black drink container
8 – the top of the clipboard the woman is holding on page 12
9 – in the pulley on page 16
10 – on the front of the cart on page 18
11 – on the bottom of the ladder on page 21
12 – between the wheels on the body of the truck that is farthest left

Internet Sites

FactHound offers a safe, fun way to find Internet sites related to this book. All of the sites on FactHound have been researched by our staff.
Here's all you do:
Visit *www.facthound.com*
Type in this code: 9781404862944

Datos divertidos

 Antes de construir cualquier cosa, es preciso sacar la tierra para hacer los cimientos del edificio. ¡Los cimientos sostienen a todo el edificio!

 La estructura más alta del mundo, que se sostiene por sí sola, es la Torre CN en Toronto, Canadá. ¡Esta torre tiene 1,815 pies (533 metros) de altura!

 Se necesitan muchas personas para construir un edificio completo. Incluyen carpinteros, electricistas, plomeros, pintores y muchos otros.

Encuentra los números

Ahora que ya terminaste de leer el cuento, aún te espera una sorpresa. En cada ilustración se encuentra escondido un número del 1 al 12. ¿Puedes encontrarlos a todos?

1 – la ventana a la mitad del primer piso del plano
2 – listo para extraerse por la pala de la derecha
3 – en la rueda delantera del camión más a la derecha
4 – justo debajo del carrete del cable en el martinete de la extrema izquierda
5 – en la bota del trabajador que está vaciando el cemento de su camión
6 – en la parte de arriba del cable de la grúa
7 – en el asa del frasco azul y negro
8 – en la parte de arriba del portapapeles que sostiene la mujer en la página 12
9 – en la polea en la página 16
10 – en el frente del carro en la página 18
11 – debajo de la escalera en la página 21
12 – entre las ruedas del camión en la extrema izquierda

Sitios de Internet

FactHound brinda una forma segura y divertida de encontrar sitios de Internet relacionados con este libro. Todos los sitios en FactHound han sido investigados por nuestro personal.
Esto es todo lo que tienes que hacer:
Visita *www.facthound.com*
Ingresa este código: 9781404862944

WITHDRAWAL